Copyright © 2023 by B. R. Breathing (Author)
All rights reserved. No part of this book may be reproduced or utilized in any form or by any means, electronic or mechanical, including photocopying, recording or by any information storage and retrieval system, without permission in writing from the publisher, except for brief quotations in critical articles or reviews.

The content of this book is based on various sources and is intended for educational and entertainment purposes only. While the author has made every effort to ensure the accuracy, completeness, and reliability of the information provided, the information may be subject to errors, omissions, or inaccuracies. Therefore, the author makes no warranties, express or implied, regarding the content of this book.

Readers are advised to seek the guidance of a licensed professional before attempting any techniques or actions outlined in this book. The author is not responsible for any losses, damages, or injuries that may arise from the use of information contained within. The information provided in this book is not intended to be a substitute for professional advice, and readers should not rely solely on the information presented.

By reading this book, readers acknowledge that the author is not providing legal, financial, medical, or professional advice. Any reliance on the information contained in this book is solely at the reader's own risk.

Thank you for selecting this book as a valuable source of knowledge and inspiration. Our aim is to provide you with insights and information that will enrich your understanding and enhance your personal growth. We appreciate your decision to embark on this journey of discovery with us, and we hope that this book will exceed your expectations and leave a lasting impact on your life.

Title: Mindfulness-Based Stress Reduction: Finding Relief from Anxiety and Tension
Subtitle: Simple and Effective Techniques for Managing Stress and Cultivating Resilience

Series: The Mindful Life Series: Cultivating Awareness and Connection in Everyday Living
Author: B. R. Breathing

Table of Contents

Introduction 6
   What is mindfulness-based stress reduction (MBSR)? 6
   The benefits of MBSR for mental and emotional well-being 9
   How MBSR can help manage stress 12

Chapter 1: Understanding Stress 15
   What is stress? 15
   The different types of stress 18
   The effects of stress on mental and physical health 21
   The role of mindfulness in reducing stress 23

Chapter 2: The MBSR Program 26
   The history of MBSR 26
   The structure of an MBSR program 28
   The key components of an MBSR program 31
   The benefits of participating in an MBSR program 34

Chapter 3: Mindful Breathing Exercises 37
   The importance of breath awareness in stress reduction 37
   Techniques for practicing mindful breathing 39
   The benefits of mindful breathing exercises 42
   Incorporating mindful breathing into daily life 45

Chapter 4: Body Scan Meditation 48
   What is a body scan meditation? 48

Techniques for practicing a body scan meditation 50
The benefits of body scan meditation 53
Incorporating body scan meditation into daily life 56

Chapter 5: Mindful Movement 58
The benefits of mindful movement for stress reduction .. 58
Yoga as a form of mindful movement 61
Techniques for practicing mindful movement 64
Incorporating mindful movement into daily life 66

Chapter 6: Developing Mindful Awareness 69
The importance of mindful awareness in stress reduction 69
Techniques for developing mindful awareness 73
The benefits of mindful awareness 76
Incorporating mindful awareness into daily life 78

Chapter 7: Cultivating Compassion 81
The importance of compassion in stress reduction 81
Techniques for developing self-compassion 84
Techniques for developing compassion for others 88
The benefits of cultivating compassion 91

Conclusion 94
The benefits of MBSR for mental and emotional well-being 94
Encouragement to continue practicing mindfulness-based stress reduction 97

Further resources for exploring MBSR and mindfulness
.... *99*
Wordbook **105**
Supplementary Materials **107**

Introduction
What is mindfulness-based stress reduction (MBSR)?

Stress is an inevitable part of life, and it can have a significant impact on our mental and physical well-being. While it's impossible to eliminate all sources of stress, there are strategies we can use to manage it more effectively. Mindfulness-based stress reduction (MBSR) is one such strategy that has gained popularity in recent years. In this section, we'll explore what MBSR is and how it can help us manage stress.

What is mindfulness-based stress reduction (MBSR)?

MBSR is a structured program that combines mindfulness meditation, body awareness, and yoga to help people manage stress, anxiety, and other chronic conditions. It was developed by Jon Kabat-Zinn, a professor of medicine emeritus at the University of Massachusetts Medical School, in the late 1970s.

The program was initially designed for patients with chronic pain, but it has since been adapted to help individuals cope with a wide range of conditions, including stress, anxiety, depression, and insomnia. MBSR is based on the idea that by cultivating mindfulness – a state of non-judgmental awareness of the present moment – we can learn to respond more effectively to stressors in our lives.

The benefits of MBSR for mental and emotional well-being

Research has shown that MBSR can have a range of benefits for mental and emotional well-being. For example, a systematic review of 29 randomized controlled trials found that MBSR was effective in reducing symptoms of anxiety and depression in people with a variety of medical and psychiatric conditions (Hofmann et al., 2010).

Other studies have found that MBSR can improve attention and cognitive functioning, reduce emotional reactivity, and increase overall well-being (Carmody & Baer, 2008; Creswell et al., 2007; Khoury et al., 2015).

How MBSR can help manage stress

MBSR can be an effective tool for managing stress because it helps us develop the skills we need to cope with stressors more effectively. Through mindfulness meditation, we learn to observe our thoughts and feelings without getting caught up in them. We also learn to focus our attention on the present moment, rather than ruminating on past or future events.

Body awareness practices, such as body scan meditation and mindful movement, help us become more attuned to the physical sensations of stress in our bodies. By learning to notice and release tension, we can reduce the physiological effects of stress and promote relaxation.

Yoga is another important component of MBSR. Yoga poses, or asanas, help us release physical tension and promote relaxation. Yoga also incorporates breathing techniques, which can be helpful in reducing the physiological effects of stress.

Conclusion

MBSR is a structured program that combines mindfulness meditation, body awareness, and yoga to help individuals manage stress and other chronic conditions. Research has shown that MBSR can have a range of benefits for mental and emotional well-being, including reducing symptoms of anxiety and depression and improving overall well-being. By cultivating mindfulness, body awareness, and yoga, we can develop the skills we need to cope with stressors more effectively and promote relaxation and well-being in our lives.

The benefits of MBSR for mental and emotional well-being

MBSR, or mindfulness-based stress reduction, is a practice that has gained a lot of attention in recent years due to its numerous benefits for mental and emotional well-being. The practice of MBSR involves developing mindfulness skills through a structured program that includes practices such as mindful breathing exercises, body scan meditations, and yoga.

The benefits of MBSR for mental and emotional well-being are extensive, and research has shown that regular practice of MBSR can have a positive impact on a range of mental health conditions, including anxiety, depression, and stress-related disorders. In this section, we will explore the benefits of MBSR in greater detail.

One of the primary benefits of MBSR is stress reduction. Stress is a pervasive problem in modern society, and it can have a significant impact on mental and physical health. Chronic stress has been linked to a range of health problems, including cardiovascular disease, diabetes, and mental health disorders. MBSR can help to reduce stress levels by providing individuals with the tools and techniques they need to manage their stress effectively.

MBSR has also been shown to be effective in reducing symptoms of anxiety and depression. Anxiety and depression are two of the most common mental health disorders, and they can have a significant impact on an individual's quality of life. Studies have shown that MBSR can be an effective treatment for these conditions, helping individuals to manage their symptoms and improve their overall well-being.

In addition to reducing stress, anxiety, and depression, MBSR can also improve emotional regulation. Emotional regulation refers to an individual's ability to manage their emotions effectively, and it is an important aspect of mental and emotional well-being. Studies have shown that regular practice of MBSR can improve emotional regulation, helping individuals to manage difficult emotions and improve their overall mood.

Another benefit of MBSR is improved cognitive function. Research has shown that regular practice of mindfulness can improve cognitive function, including attention, memory, and decision-making. These benefits can be particularly important for individuals who are dealing with stress or mental health issues, as they can help to improve overall functioning and quality of life.

Finally, MBSR can help to promote overall well-being by providing individuals with a greater sense of purpose and meaning. The practice of mindfulness can help individuals to develop a greater awareness of their thoughts and feelings, and to connect more deeply with their inner selves. This can lead to a greater sense of purpose and meaning in life, helping individuals to feel more fulfilled and satisfied overall.

In summary, the benefits of MBSR for mental and emotional well-being are extensive, and research has shown that regular practice of MBSR can have a positive impact on a range of mental health conditions, including stress, anxiety, depression, and more. By providing individuals with the tools and techniques they need to manage their emotions effectively, MBSR can help to improve overall well-being and quality of life.

How MBSR can help manage stress

Stress is a common problem in modern society, and it can have a significant impact on mental and physical health. The practice of mindfulness-based stress reduction (MBSR) is a technique that can help individuals manage stress more effectively. In this section, we will explore how MBSR can help manage stress.

MBSR is a structured program that teaches individuals how to develop mindfulness skills. Mindfulness involves being present and fully engaged in the present moment, without judgment or distraction. The practice of mindfulness can help individuals to manage stress by providing them with the tools and techniques they need to be more present and aware in their daily lives.

One of the key ways that MBSR can help manage stress is by reducing the body's stress response. When the body experiences stress, it releases hormones such as cortisol and adrenaline, which can lead to a range of physical symptoms, including increased heart rate, rapid breathing, and muscle tension. These symptoms can be uncomfortable and can make it difficult for individuals to manage stress effectively.

MBSR can help to reduce the body's stress response by promoting relaxation and reducing muscle tension.

Practices such as mindful breathing exercises and body scan meditations can help individuals to become more aware of their physical sensations and to release tension in their muscles. This can help to reduce the physical symptoms of stress and promote feelings of relaxation and calm.

In addition to reducing the body's stress response, MBSR can also help individuals to manage their thoughts and emotions more effectively. When individuals are stressed, they may experience a range of negative thoughts and emotions, such as worry, fear, and anxiety. These thoughts and emotions can be overwhelming and can make it difficult for individuals to manage their stress effectively.

The practice of mindfulness can help individuals to manage their thoughts and emotions by promoting awareness and acceptance. Rather than trying to suppress or avoid negative thoughts and emotions, mindfulness encourages individuals to observe them non-judgmentally and to let them pass without getting caught up in them. This can help individuals to manage their stress more effectively and to develop a more positive outlook on life.

Finally, MBSR can help individuals to develop a greater sense of resilience in the face of stress. Resilience refers to an individual's ability to bounce back from difficult experiences and to adapt to new situations. By promoting awareness, acceptance, and relaxation, MBSR can help individuals to develop greater resilience and to cope more effectively with the challenges of daily life.

In summary, MBSR can help individuals to manage stress by promoting relaxation, reducing the body's stress response, and helping individuals to manage their thoughts and emotions more effectively. By promoting awareness and acceptance, MBSR can help individuals to develop a greater sense of resilience and to cope more effectively with the challenges of daily life.

Chapter 1: Understanding Stress
What is stress?

Stress is a natural response of the body to a perceived threat, challenge or demand. It is a physiological and psychological reaction that prepares the body to deal with situations that require an immediate response. Stress is a normal part of life, and everyone experiences it from time to time. However, chronic stress can have negative effects on our physical, mental, and emotional well-being.

There are different types of stress, including acute stress, episodic acute stress, and chronic stress. Acute stress is the most common type and is usually short-lived. It is the body's immediate response to a perceived threat or challenge, and it can be beneficial in small doses, as it can help us focus and stay alert. For example, when we encounter a dangerous situation, such as a car accident, our body responds by releasing adrenaline, which helps us react quickly and effectively.

Episodic acute stress is a more frequent form of stress. It is often experienced by people who are constantly overwhelmed by the demands of daily life, such as work deadlines, financial pressures, and relationship problems. People who experience episodic acute stress often feel like they are in a perpetual state of crisis, and they may become irritable, anxious, or depressed.

Chronic stress is the most damaging form of stress. It occurs when a person is exposed to prolonged or repeated stressors, such as job dissatisfaction, financial problems, or relationship conflicts. Chronic stress can lead to a range of physical and mental health problems, including high blood pressure, heart disease, diabetes, depression, anxiety, and insomnia.

Stress can be caused by many different factors, including external events, such as work pressures, family conflicts, and financial problems, as well as internal factors, such as negative thoughts, beliefs, and emotions. The body's response to stress involves the release of stress hormones, such as cortisol and adrenaline, which trigger a range of physiological changes, including increased heart rate, blood pressure, and respiration.

The impact of stress on mental health is also significant. Chronic stress can lead to depression, anxiety disorders, and other mental health problems. It can also contribute to cognitive problems such as memory impairment and difficulty concentrating.

In summary, stress is a natural response to a perceived threat, challenge, or demand. While acute stress can be beneficial in small doses, chronic stress can have negative effects on our physical, mental, and emotional well-being. Understanding stress is the first step in learning how to manage it effectively.

The different types of stress

Stress is a normal part of everyday life, and it can manifest in many different ways. Not all stress is bad, and in fact, some types of stress can be motivating and even beneficial. However, prolonged or chronic stress can have a negative impact on mental and physical health. In order to better understand stress and its effects, it is important to recognize the different types of stress that people may experience.

1. Acute Stress Acute stress is a type of stress that is short-lived and typically occurs in response to a specific event or situation. Examples of acute stress include taking an exam, giving a presentation, or getting into a car accident. While acute stress can be unpleasant, it is usually temporary and doesn't have long-lasting effects on health.

2. Chronic Stress Chronic stress is ongoing stress that persists over a long period of time. It can result from a variety of sources, such as a demanding job, financial problems, or relationship issues. Chronic stress can lead to a range of physical and mental health problems, including anxiety, depression, heart disease, and obesity.

3. Eustress Eustress is a type of stress that is positive and motivating. It is typically associated with challenging but achievable goals or situations, such as training for a

marathon or starting a new job. Eustress can increase motivation and productivity, and can even be enjoyable.

4. Distress Distress is a type of stress that is negative and overwhelming. It can be caused by a variety of factors, including major life changes, trauma, or ongoing difficulties at work or home. Distress can lead to a range of physical and mental health problems, including chronic anxiety, depression, and post-traumatic stress disorder (PTSD).

5. Traumatic Stress Traumatic stress is a type of stress that is caused by a traumatic event, such as experiencing or witnessing a natural disaster, being a victim of violence, or serving in combat. Traumatic stress can lead to a range of physical and mental health problems, including PTSD.

6. Secondary Traumatic Stress Secondary traumatic stress is a type of stress that is experienced by people who are exposed to traumatic events or trauma survivors, such as first responders, healthcare workers, or therapists. It can lead to a range of physical and mental health problems, including compassion fatigue and burnout.

In summary, stress is a natural part of life, but it can become problematic if it persists over a long period of time or if it is overwhelming. By recognizing the different types of stress that people may experience, it is possible to better understand the effects of stress and to develop strategies for managing it.

The effects of stress on mental and physical health

Stress is a natural and normal response to the challenges we face in our lives. However, when stress becomes chronic or overwhelming, it can have serious negative effects on both our mental and physical health. In this section, we will explore the different ways in which stress can impact our well-being.

Mental Health Effects of Stress

1. Anxiety: Chronic stress can lead to increased anxiety and worry. This can manifest in physical symptoms such as restlessness, difficulty concentrating, and irritability.

2. Depression: Research has shown a link between chronic stress and depression. Prolonged stress can lead to feelings of hopelessness and a loss of interest in activities that were once enjoyable.

3. Mood Swings: Stress can cause significant changes in mood, leading to irritability, anger, and frustration. It can also make it difficult to regulate emotions and manage stress.

4. Cognitive Functioning: Chronic stress can impair cognitive functioning, leading to memory problems and difficulty concentrating.

Physical Health Effects of Stress

1. Cardiovascular Health: Prolonged stress can increase blood pressure and heart rate, leading to a greater risk of heart disease.

2. Digestive Health: Chronic stress can lead to digestive problems such as irritable bowel syndrome and stomach ulcers.

3. Immune System: Stress can suppress the immune system, making individuals more susceptible to illness and infection.

4. Chronic Pain: Stress can exacerbate chronic pain conditions such as migraines, back pain, and arthritis.

Overall, the negative effects of stress on our mental and physical health can be significant. Mindfulness-based stress reduction can be an effective tool for managing stress and mitigating its negative effects. By learning to recognize and regulate our stress responses, we can improve our well-being and overall quality of life.

The role of mindfulness in reducing stress

Mindfulness has gained increasing popularity as a tool for reducing stress and promoting well-being. Mindfulness is a practice that involves paying attention to the present moment, with an attitude of curiosity, openness, and non-judgment. When practiced regularly, mindfulness can help reduce the negative effects of stress on mental and physical health.

Mindfulness-based stress reduction (MBSR) is a specific program that combines mindfulness meditation, gentle yoga, and other mindfulness practices to help individuals cope with stress. The MBSR program was developed in the 1970s by Dr. Jon Kabat-Zinn at the University of Massachusetts Medical School.

Research has shown that practicing mindfulness can have a number of benefits for mental and physical health, including reducing stress and anxiety, improving mood, enhancing cognitive function, and reducing symptoms of depression. Mindfulness has also been found to have a positive impact on physical health, including reducing blood pressure, improving sleep quality, and reducing chronic pain.

So how does mindfulness reduce stress? One way is by increasing our ability to regulate our emotions. Mindfulness can help us become more aware of our thoughts, feelings, and physical sensations, which in turn can help us identify when we are experiencing stress and take steps to address it. By becoming more aware of our thoughts and feelings, we can begin to identify patterns of negative thinking that may be contributing to our stress and learn to shift our focus to more positive and productive thoughts.

Mindfulness can also help us develop a greater sense of self-awareness, which can help us identify our personal triggers for stress. By becoming more aware of what triggers our stress, we can take steps to avoid or manage these situations more effectively. This can include practicing relaxation techniques, such as deep breathing or progressive muscle relaxation, or engaging in activities that promote relaxation, such as yoga or meditation.

In addition, mindfulness can help us develop greater resilience in the face of stress. By becoming more present and aware in each moment, we can learn to approach challenges with greater clarity and focus, and develop a greater sense of acceptance and compassion for ourselves and others.

Overall, the practice of mindfulness can be a powerful tool for reducing stress and promoting overall well-being. By cultivating greater awareness and self-compassion, we can learn to manage stress more effectively and develop greater resilience in the face of life's challenges.

Chapter 2: The MBSR Program
The history of MBSR

The history of MBSR dates back to the late 1970s, when Dr. Jon Kabat-Zinn, a molecular biologist and meditation teacher, developed the program at the University of Massachusetts Medical School. At the time, there was a growing interest in alternative approaches to healthcare, and mindfulness-based practices were gaining attention for their potential to alleviate a wide range of health issues, including chronic pain, anxiety, and depression.

Kabat-Zinn was inspired by his own experience with mindfulness meditation, which he had learned while studying with Buddhist teachers. He believed that mindfulness could be used as a tool for managing stress and improving overall well-being, and he set out to create a program that would make mindfulness accessible to a wider audience.

The initial MBSR program was designed to help individuals with chronic pain, but Kabat-Zinn quickly realized that it could be beneficial for anyone dealing with stress and related issues. The program was based on a combination of mindfulness meditation, yoga, and mind-body awareness, and it was delivered in a structured eight-week format.

The early days of MBSR were met with some skepticism, as many people were unfamiliar with mindfulness and skeptical of its potential benefits. However, as more research was conducted on the program, and as more people began to experience its benefits firsthand, interest in MBSR grew.

Today, MBSR is widely recognized as an evidence-based intervention for stress reduction and other mental health issues. The program has been adapted and modified for use in a variety of settings, including healthcare, education, and corporate wellness programs, and it continues to be studied and refined by researchers and practitioners around the world.

The structure of an MBSR program

The structure of an MBSR program is designed to guide participants through a process of learning and developing mindfulness skills, with the ultimate goal of reducing stress and promoting overall well-being. While the specifics of each MBSR program may vary depending on the instructor and setting, there are generally several core components that are essential to the program.

Orientation and Introduction: The first session of an MBSR program typically involves an orientation and introduction to the program. The instructor will provide an overview of what the program entails, what participants can expect, and answer any questions that participants may have.

Weekly Group Sessions: MBSR programs typically involve weekly group sessions that last between 2-3 hours. During these sessions, participants will engage in various mindfulness practices, such as meditation, yoga, and body scans. There will also be time for group discussion and reflection on the challenges and benefits of practicing mindfulness.

Home Practice: In addition to attending the weekly group sessions, participants are encouraged to engage in daily home practice of mindfulness exercises. This may include formal meditation practices, such as breath awareness or body scan meditations, as well as informal practices, such as mindful breathing during daily activities.

All-Day Silent Retreat: Most MBSR programs include an all-day silent retreat, which typically occurs between weeks six and seven of the program. During the retreat, participants engage in extended periods of mindfulness practice and reflection, with minimal interaction or communication with others.

The MBSR Curriculum: The MBSR curriculum consists of a series of mindfulness practices and exercises designed to help participants develop greater awareness of their thoughts, emotions, and physical sensations, and to cultivate a sense of non-judgmental acceptance and compassion. The curriculum may include a range of practices, such as body scan meditations, mindful breathing exercises, and mindful movement practices, such as yoga.

Individualized Support: While MBSR is primarily a group-based program, participants may also have access to individualized support from the instructor, such as one-on-one meetings or check-ins to discuss their progress and address any questions or concerns.

Overall, the structure of an MBSR program is designed to provide participants with a supportive and structured environment in which to learn and practice mindfulness skills, and to develop the capacity for greater self-awareness, self-compassion, and stress reduction.

The key components of an MBSR program

The key components of an MBSR program involve a structured approach to mindfulness-based stress reduction. This approach has been carefully designed to ensure that participants get the maximum benefits from the program. The following are some of the key components of an MBSR program:

1. Mindfulness Meditation Mindfulness meditation is a central component of the MBSR program. It involves training the mind to focus on the present moment and developing an awareness of one's thoughts, feelings, and physical sensations. This is done through guided meditations, which are led by an experienced mindfulness teacher. The aim of mindfulness meditation is to develop greater awareness and acceptance of one's internal experiences, without judgment.

2. Body Scan The body scan is another important component of the MBSR program. It involves lying down and systematically scanning the body from head to toe, paying attention to any sensations or areas of tension. The body scan is a powerful tool for developing body awareness, reducing physical tension, and improving the mind-body connection.

3. Mindful Movement In addition to mindfulness meditation and the body scan, the MBSR program also includes mindful movement practices such as gentle yoga or walking meditation. These practices are designed to help participants develop greater awareness of their body and movement, as well as reduce physical tension and improve flexibility.

4. Group Support Group support is an important component of the MBSR program. Participants meet regularly in a group setting to practice mindfulness together and share their experiences. This creates a sense of community and support, and allows participants to learn from each other's experiences.

5. Homework Assignments Homework assignments are an essential part of the MBSR program. Participants are given daily mindfulness practices to do at home, such as guided meditations or mindful movement practices. These practices help to reinforce the learning and integrate mindfulness into daily life.

6. Mindful Eating Mindful eating is another important component of the MBSR program. It involves paying attention to the sensory experience of eating, such as the taste, smell, and texture of food. Mindful eating helps participants to develop a healthier relationship with food,

reduce overeating, and increase awareness of the connection between food and emotional well-being.

7. Stress Reduction Techniques The MBSR program also includes stress reduction techniques such as progressive muscle relaxation or deep breathing. These techniques are used to help participants reduce physical tension and relax the body and mind.

Overall, the key components of an MBSR program are designed to help participants develop greater awareness, reduce stress and anxiety, and improve overall well-being. By engaging in daily mindfulness practices and participating in a supportive group environment, participants can experience significant improvements in mental and physical health.

The benefits of participating in an MBSR program

Participating in a mindfulness-based stress reduction (MBSR) program has many benefits for mental and emotional well-being. In this chapter, we will explore the benefits of participating in an MBSR program and how it can positively impact your life.

1. Reduces Stress MBSR programs are specifically designed to help individuals manage stress. Studies have shown that participants in MBSR programs have reduced symptoms of anxiety and depression, decreased levels of cortisol (the stress hormone), and increased feelings of calmness and well-being. Regular practice of mindfulness has also been shown to help people cope with stressful situations more effectively.

2. Improves Physical Health Stress has a significant impact on physical health, and chronic stress has been linked to many health problems, including high blood pressure, heart disease, and obesity. By reducing stress, MBSR can have a positive impact on physical health. In fact, studies have shown that MBSR can lower blood pressure, improve immune function, and even reduce chronic pain.

3. Enhances Cognitive Function MBSR programs can improve cognitive function, including attention, memory, and decision-making skills. By practicing mindfulness,

individuals can improve their ability to focus and concentrate, which can be particularly beneficial for individuals with attention deficit hyperactivity disorder (ADHD) or other attention-related disorders.

4. Boosts Emotional Intelligence MBSR programs can also help individuals develop emotional intelligence, which is the ability to recognize, understand, and manage one's own emotions and the emotions of others. This can lead to improved communication, better relationships, and greater empathy and compassion.

5. Promotes Self-Awareness Through regular mindfulness practice, individuals can develop greater self-awareness, which is the ability to recognize one's own thoughts, emotions, and behaviors. This can lead to improved self-regulation and self-management skills, which can be particularly helpful for individuals struggling with addiction, eating disorders, or other impulse control issues.

6. Increases Resilience Finally, MBSR programs can increase resilience, which is the ability to bounce back from difficult situations and challenges. By practicing mindfulness, individuals can develop greater emotional flexibility and adaptability, which can help them cope with stress and adversity more effectively.

Overall, participating in an MBSR program can have many benefits for mental and emotional well-being. Whether you are struggling with stress, anxiety, depression, or other mental health concerns, MBSR can provide valuable tools and techniques to help you manage your symptoms and improve your quality of life.

Chapter 3: Mindful Breathing Exercises
The importance of breath awareness in stress reduction

Breath awareness is an essential aspect of mindfulness practice and can be a powerful tool for reducing stress and promoting relaxation. By bringing our attention to the sensations of our breath, we can cultivate a sense of calm and stability, which can help us manage stress more effectively.

Stress can cause our breathing to become shallow and rapid, which can exacerbate feelings of anxiety and tension. By practicing breath awareness, we can learn to regulate our breathing and bring it back into a natural rhythm. This can help to reduce the physical symptoms of stress, such as increased heart rate and muscle tension.

One of the key benefits of breath awareness is that it can be done anytime, anywhere, without the need for any special equipment or space. This makes it a convenient and accessible technique for managing stress in daily life. By simply taking a few moments to focus on our breath, we can shift our attention away from stressful thoughts and feelings and bring ourselves back to the present moment.

In addition to its immediate benefits for stress reduction, breath awareness can also have long-term benefits for our overall health and well-being. Studies have shown that regular mindfulness practice, including breath awareness, can improve immune function, lower blood pressure, and reduce symptoms of depression and anxiety.

There are many different techniques for practicing breath awareness, from simple breath counting to more complex visualization exercises. The key is to find a technique that works for you and to practice it regularly, ideally every day.

Incorporating breath awareness into our daily routines can be as simple as taking a few deep breaths before a meeting or when we feel overwhelmed, or taking a few moments to focus on our breath when we wake up or before we go to bed. Over time, these small moments of mindfulness can add up to significant improvements in our ability to manage stress and promote overall well-being.

Techniques for practicing mindful breathing

Mindful breathing is an integral part of the mindfulness-based stress reduction (MBSR) program. By paying attention to the breath and cultivating awareness of the present moment, individuals can reduce stress, calm the mind, and increase overall well-being. In this chapter, we will explore various techniques for practicing mindful breathing.

1. The Body Scan The body scan is a mindfulness exercise that involves systematically bringing awareness to different parts of the body, beginning with the toes and moving up to the head. During the body scan, individuals lie down in a comfortable position and focus on their breath. They then move their attention to their toes and become aware of any sensations, such as tension or discomfort. They then move their attention slowly up the body, focusing on each part in turn. The body scan helps individuals to develop a greater sense of awareness and connection with their body.

2. Counting Breaths Counting breaths is a simple but effective technique for practicing mindful breathing. During this exercise, individuals sit in a comfortable position and focus on their breath. They then count each inhalation and exhalation, up to a count of ten. If the mind wanders, they start again from one. Counting breaths helps to develop

focus and concentration, and can be a useful technique for those who find it difficult to sit still and quiet the mind.

3. Square Breathing Square breathing is a technique that involves breathing in for a count of four, holding the breath for a count of four, exhaling for a count of four, and then holding the breath again for a count of four, before starting the cycle again. This technique helps to slow the breath and calm the mind, and can be useful for individuals who are feeling anxious or overwhelmed.

4. Mindful Breathing Meditation The mindful breathing meditation is a core practice in the MBSR program. During this exercise, individuals sit in a comfortable position and focus on their breath. They may focus on the sensation of the breath at the nostrils or in the belly. As they breathe in, they silently say to themselves, "breathing in," and as they breathe out, they say, "breathing out." If the mind wanders, they simply acknowledge the thought and gently bring their attention back to the breath. This technique helps to develop present moment awareness and cultivates a sense of calm and relaxation.

5. Three-Part Breath The three-part breath is a technique that involves breathing into the belly, the chest, and the upper chest, in turn. During this exercise, individuals sit in a comfortable position and place their

hands on their belly. They then breathe in, filling the belly with air, and then continue to breathe in, filling the chest with air. Finally, they continue to breathe in, filling the upper chest with air. They then exhale slowly, releasing the air from the upper chest, then the chest, and finally the belly. This technique helps to develop awareness of the breath and can be useful for those who feel anxious or have difficulty breathing deeply.

In conclusion, there are various techniques for practicing mindful breathing, each with its unique benefits. By incorporating these techniques into daily practice, individuals can cultivate greater awareness and reduce stress and anxiety.

The benefits of mindful breathing exercises

Mindful breathing exercises are a key component of mindfulness-based stress reduction (MBSR) programs. The practice of mindful breathing involves paying attention to the breath in a non-judgmental way, and can have numerous benefits for both mental and physical health.

Here are some of the benefits of practicing mindful breathing exercises:

1. Reducing stress and anxiety: Mindful breathing has been shown to reduce stress and anxiety by activating the relaxation response in the body. By focusing on the breath, we can calm the mind and reduce feelings of stress and anxiety.

2. Improving emotional regulation: Mindful breathing exercises can help us to better regulate our emotions, by increasing our awareness of our emotional state and helping us to respond more skillfully to difficult emotions.

3. Increasing focus and concentration: Mindful breathing exercises require sustained attention, which can help to improve focus and concentration. By practicing mindful breathing regularly, we can develop our ability to stay present and focused in our daily lives.

4. Improving physical health: Mindful breathing has been shown to have numerous physical health benefits,

including reducing blood pressure and improving lung function. By increasing our awareness of our breath, we can also improve our posture and breathing patterns.

5. Enhancing overall well-being: Mindful breathing exercises can contribute to an overall sense of well-being by helping us to feel more present, connected, and in control of our lives.

There are many different techniques for practicing mindful breathing exercises. Here are a few examples:

1. Basic breath awareness: This involves simply paying attention to the breath as it moves in and out of the body. You can focus your attention on the sensations of the breath at the nostrils, chest, or abdomen.

2. Counting the breath: This involves counting each inhale and exhale, up to a certain number (e.g. 10), and then starting over again. This can help to keep the mind focused on the breath.

3. Lengthening the breath: This involves intentionally lengthening the inhalation and exhalation, for example by inhaling for a count of four and exhaling for a count of six.

4. Noting the breath: This involves mentally noting each inhale and exhale with a simple label, such as "in" and "out." This can help to increase awareness of the breath and reduce distractions.

Overall, practicing mindful breathing exercises can have numerous benefits for mental and physical health. By incorporating these exercises into our daily routine, we can improve our overall well-being and reduce feelings of stress and anxiety.

Incorporating mindful breathing into daily life

Incorporating mindful breathing exercises into daily life can be a powerful tool for reducing stress and increasing overall well-being. Here are some techniques and tips for incorporating mindful breathing exercises into your daily routine.

1. Start with short, frequent practice sessions It can be difficult to find time for a long meditation practice in the midst of a busy day, so start with short, frequent sessions of mindful breathing. Set a timer for 1-5 minutes and focus on your breath during that time. As you become more comfortable with the practice, you can gradually increase the length of your sessions.

2. Make use of reminders Set reminders throughout your day to practice mindful breathing. This can be as simple as setting an alarm on your phone to go off every hour or putting up a sticky note on your computer monitor or fridge. These reminders can help you remember to take a few moments to focus on your breath and bring your attention back to the present moment.

3. Practice mindful breathing during daily activities You don't have to be sitting in a quiet room to practice mindful breathing. You can incorporate this technique into your daily activities, such as taking a shower, walking the

dog, or cooking dinner. Use these moments to focus on your breath and bring your attention back to the present moment.

4. Practice while waiting We spend a lot of time waiting throughout the day, whether it's waiting in line at the grocery store or waiting for a meeting to start. Use these moments of waiting to practice mindful breathing. Focus on your breath and use the time to bring your attention back to the present moment.

5. Use mindful breathing to transition between activities Mindful breathing can be a useful tool for transitioning between activities throughout the day. Take a few moments to focus on your breath before starting a new task or after finishing one. This can help you clear your mind and approach the next task with renewed focus and energy.

6. Create a routine Incorporating mindful breathing into your daily routine can help make it a habit. Find a time that works for you, such as first thing in the morning or before bed, and make it a regular part of your day. This routine can help you make the practice a priority and ensure that you're getting the benefits of mindful breathing on a regular basis.

Incorporating mindful breathing exercises into your daily routine can help reduce stress, increase focus and productivity, and improve overall well-being. With a little practice and persistence, you can make this technique a habit and reap the benefits in your daily life.

Chapter 4: Body Scan Meditation
What is a body scan meditation?

Body scan meditation is a mindfulness-based stress reduction (MBSR) technique that involves a systematic and intentional focus on different parts of the body. It is a form of guided meditation that aims to bring attention to bodily sensations, emotions, and thoughts in a non-judgmental way. By practicing body scan meditation, one can increase self-awareness, reduce stress, and promote relaxation.

At its core, body scan meditation involves intentionally focusing on one part of the body at a time, moving sequentially from the top of the head to the tips of the toes. The purpose of this practice is to bring awareness to the different sensations that arise in each part of the body. The practice can be done in a sitting or lying-down position, and the guided meditation can range from 10 to 45 minutes, depending on the practitioner's preference and experience.

During the body scan meditation, the practitioner is instructed to pay attention to the sensations, thoughts, and emotions that arise without judgment. The goal is to simply observe and acknowledge what is happening in the body, rather than trying to change or control it. By doing so, one can become more attuned to bodily sensations and more present in the moment, leading to a reduction in stress and anxiety.

The body scan meditation is often described as a form of "moving meditation" because it involves intentionally moving one's attention through different parts of the body. As such, it is a more active form of meditation compared to traditional mindfulness practices that involve sitting still and focusing on the breath. However, the movement involved in body scan meditation is internal rather than external, making it accessible to people of all physical abilities.

The body scan meditation is a practice that has been used in many different contexts, including in clinical settings to help individuals cope with chronic pain, anxiety, depression, and other mental health conditions. It has also been used in corporate wellness programs to promote mindfulness, reduce stress, and improve overall well-being among employees.

Overall, body scan meditation is a powerful tool for increasing self-awareness, reducing stress, and promoting relaxation. By practicing this technique regularly, individuals can learn to better connect with their bodies, manage their emotions, and experience a greater sense of well-being.

Techniques for practicing a body scan meditation

Body scan meditation is a mindfulness technique that involves paying attention to the physical sensations in your body. The practice is typically done while lying down, but it can also be done while seated. The goal of the body scan is to develop awareness of your body and its sensations, which can help you become more present and reduce stress.

Here are some techniques for practicing a body scan meditation:

1. Find a quiet place to practice: Choose a quiet space where you won't be disturbed. It's also helpful to turn off your phone and other electronics to minimize distractions.

2. Get comfortable: Lie down on your back on a yoga mat or comfortable surface, with your legs uncrossed and your arms at your sides. If you have trouble lying flat, you can place a pillow under your knees to support your lower back.

3. Focus on your breath: Take a few deep breaths to relax and bring your attention to the present moment. Then, allow your breath to settle into its natural rhythm, and bring your attention to your body.

4. Scan your body: Start at the top of your head and slowly scan down your body, paying attention to each part of

your body in turn. Notice any sensations you feel in each area, such as tension, warmth, or tingling.

5. Stay present: If your mind starts to wander, gently bring your attention back to the present moment and the sensations in your body. Don't judge or analyze your thoughts, just observe them and let them pass.

6. Practice regularly: Consistency is key when it comes to developing a mindfulness practice. Aim to practice a body scan meditation for 10-15 minutes each day, or as often as you can.

7. Adjust the length of your scan: As you become more comfortable with the practice, you can lengthen the time you spend scanning each part of your body. You may find that you need more time to fully tune in to the sensations in each area.

8. Experiment with different techniques: There are many variations of the body scan meditation, such as focusing on specific areas of the body or using guided meditations. Experiment with different techniques to find what works best for you.

By practicing a body scan meditation regularly, you can develop a greater awareness of your body and its sensations. This increased awareness can help you identify areas of tension or discomfort and work to release them, leading to greater physical and emotional well-being.

The benefits of body scan meditation

Body scan meditation is a powerful technique that can provide a wide range of benefits to those who practice it regularly. Here are some of the most significant benefits of body scan meditation:

1. Stress reduction: Body scan meditation is an effective tool for reducing stress and promoting relaxation. As you move your attention through your body, you can release tension and let go of stress that you may not even be aware of. This can help you feel more calm and centered, and reduce symptoms of stress such as anxiety, irritability, and insomnia.

2. Improved body awareness: Many people go through life without really being in touch with their bodies. Body scan meditation helps you become more aware of sensations in your body, both pleasant and unpleasant. This heightened body awareness can help you detect early signs of illness or injury, and improve your ability to take care of your body and respond to its needs.

3. Emotional regulation: Our bodies hold onto emotions, and sometimes we may not even be aware of this. Body scan meditation can help you tune into your body's emotional landscape, and become more aware of emotions that may be stored in different parts of your body. This

awareness can help you process and release these emotions, leading to greater emotional regulation and balance.

4. Better sleep: Body scan meditation can be a powerful tool for improving the quality of your sleep. By reducing stress and promoting relaxation, body scan meditation can help you fall asleep faster, stay asleep longer, and wake up feeling more refreshed and energized.

5. Pain relief: Body scan meditation can help reduce chronic pain and other physical discomforts. By focusing on sensations in different parts of your body, you can develop greater awareness of the location and intensity of pain, which can help you manage it more effectively. Additionally, the relaxation and stress reduction benefits of body scan meditation can help reduce tension in the body, which can further reduce pain.

6. Improved focus and concentration: Body scan meditation requires focused attention, which can help improve your ability to concentrate and stay focused on tasks. This can be especially helpful for people who struggle with distractibility or have difficulty focusing for long periods of time.

7. Increased self-awareness: Body scan meditation can help you become more aware of your thoughts, feelings, and physical sensations. This increased self-awareness can help

you better understand yourself, your reactions to different situations, and how you can make changes to improve your overall well-being.

Overall, body scan meditation is a powerful technique that can help you reduce stress, improve your physical and emotional awareness, and enhance your overall well-being. By practicing regularly, you can experience these benefits and more, and develop a greater sense of calm, clarity, and resilience in your daily life.

Incorporating body scan meditation into daily life

Body scan meditation is a powerful tool for reducing stress and promoting relaxation, but it can be challenging to incorporate it into daily life. Here are some tips for making body scan meditation a regular part of your routine:

1. Set aside time each day: One of the most important things you can do to make body scan meditation a habit is to set aside time for it each day. Whether it's 10 minutes in the morning or 20 minutes before bed, having a regular time for your practice will help you stick with it.

2. Create a peaceful environment: Find a quiet, peaceful place where you can practice your body scan meditation without distraction. This might mean turning off your phone, closing the door, or finding a comfortable spot in nature.

3. Start small: If you're new to body scan meditation, it's important to start small and work your way up. Begin with just a few minutes each day, and gradually increase the length of your practice as you become more comfortable with it.

4. Use guided meditations: Guided meditations can be helpful for beginners, as they provide structure and guidance for your practice. There are many apps and websites that

offer guided body scan meditations, so experiment with different options to find one that resonates with you.

5. Be patient: Body scan meditation is a skill, and like any skill, it takes time and practice to master. Don't get discouraged if you don't notice immediate results. Stick with it, and over time, you'll start to see the benefits.

6. Integrate into your day: Find ways to integrate body scan meditation into your daily routine. You might practice while lying in bed before getting up in the morning, or while sitting on your lunch break at work. The more you make it a part of your everyday life, the easier it will be to stick with it.

7. Be consistent: Consistency is key when it comes to meditation. Try to practice your body scan meditation at the same time and in the same place each day. This will help you establish a routine and make it easier to stick with your practice.

Incorporating body scan meditation into your daily life can have numerous benefits for your mental and physical health. With a little patience, practice, and consistency, you can make body scan meditation a regular part of your routine and enjoy the benefits of reduced stress and increased relaxation.

Chapter 5: Mindful Movement
The benefits of mindful movement for stress reduction

Mindful movement is a form of exercise that combines physical activity with mindfulness, the practice of paying attention to the present moment with a non-judgmental attitude. It is a way to cultivate awareness of the body, thoughts, and emotions, and to develop a sense of connection between the mind and body.

There is a growing body of research that suggests that practicing mindful movement can have a range of benefits for mental and physical health, including stress reduction. In this chapter, we will explore the benefits of mindful movement for stress reduction.

1. Reduces Stress and Anxiety

Mindful movement can help reduce stress and anxiety by promoting relaxation and reducing muscle tension. When we engage in physical activity, our body produces endorphins, which are chemicals that promote feelings of happiness and well-being. Mindful movement also allows us to focus on our body and breath, which can help reduce feelings of anxiety and tension.

2. Promotes Better Sleep

Stress can interfere with sleep, leading to insomnia and other sleep disorders. Mindful movement can help reduce stress, allowing us to sleep more soundly. Additionally, engaging in physical activity during the day can help regulate our sleep-wake cycle, making it easier to fall asleep at night.

3. Boosts Mood

Mindful movement can help boost mood by increasing the production of endorphins, which are known to promote feelings of happiness and well-being. Additionally, engaging in physical activity can help reduce feelings of depression and anxiety, allowing us to feel more positive and energized.

4. Increases Mind-Body Awareness

Mindful movement encourages us to pay attention to the sensations in our body, helping us to develop a greater awareness of our physical and emotional state. This awareness can help us recognize when we are experiencing stress, allowing us to take steps to manage it before it becomes overwhelming.

5. Improves Physical Health

Mindful movement can also have physical health benefits, such as reducing the risk of heart disease, diabetes, and obesity. Additionally, it can improve our balance, flexibility, and strength, making it easier to perform everyday tasks.

6. Provides a Sense of Connection

Mindful movement can be done alone or in a group, providing a sense of connection with others. Practicing with others can create a sense of community, allowing us to feel supported and encouraged.

In conclusion, mindful movement can be a valuable tool for stress reduction. It can help promote relaxation, reduce anxiety, boost mood, increase mind-body awareness, improve physical health, and provide a sense of connection. Incorporating mindful movement into our daily routine can help us manage stress and improve our overall well-being.

Yoga as a form of mindful movement

Yoga is a popular form of mindful movement that involves a series of physical postures, breathing exercises, and meditation techniques. The practice of yoga has been shown to have numerous benefits for both physical and mental health, including reducing stress and anxiety.

The word yoga comes from the Sanskrit word "yuj," which means to unite or yoke. The practice of yoga aims to unite the body, mind, and spirit, and it has been used for thousands of years as a tool for spiritual growth and self-realization. In recent years, yoga has become increasingly popular in Western countries as a form of exercise and stress reduction.

Yoga postures, or asanas, are designed to stretch, strengthen, and balance the body. They can range from simple poses such as downward-facing dog to more complex postures such as headstands and backbends. Each pose is typically held for several breaths, allowing the practitioner to focus on the sensations in the body and cultivate a sense of present-moment awareness.

In addition to physical postures, yoga also incorporates breathing techniques, or pranayama, which are designed to calm the mind and reduce stress. Pranayama techniques can include deep belly breathing, alternate nostril breathing, and breath retention exercises.

Meditation is another key component of yoga practice, and it involves training the mind to focus and quiet the constant chatter of thoughts. Meditation techniques used in yoga can include mantra repetition, visualization, and mindfulness meditation.

The benefits of yoga for stress reduction have been well-documented in research studies. A 2016 systematic review and meta-analysis of 25 randomized controlled trials found that yoga practice was associated with reduced stress, anxiety, and depression symptoms, as well as improved overall quality of life. Another study published in the Journal of Clinical Psychology in 2017 found that practicing yoga was associated with reduced perceived stress and greater resilience to stress.

One reason why yoga may be effective for reducing stress is that it activates the body's relaxation response, which is the opposite of the stress response. The relaxation response is characterized by a decrease in heart rate, blood pressure, and breathing rate, as well as a feeling of calm and relaxation.

Another benefit of yoga is that it promotes mindfulness, which can help individuals become more aware of their thoughts, feelings, and bodily sensations. This increased awareness can help individuals to identify and respond to stress in more constructive ways, rather than reacting automatically and impulsively.

Incorporating yoga into daily life can be relatively easy, as it requires minimal equipment and can be practiced almost anywhere. Many yoga studios offer classes for individuals of all levels, from beginners to advanced practitioners. Online yoga classes and instructional videos are also widely available and can be accessed from the comfort of one's own home.

In conclusion, yoga is a powerful form of mindful movement that can be an effective tool for reducing stress and anxiety. By combining physical postures, breathing techniques, and meditation practices, yoga promotes relaxation, mindfulness, and a sense of overall well-being. Incorporating yoga into daily life can be a simple and effective way to manage stress and improve mental health.

Techniques for practicing mindful movement

When it comes to practicing mindful movement, there are various techniques that can be utilized. These techniques aim to help individuals increase their body awareness, reduce stress, and promote relaxation. Here are some techniques for practicing mindful movement:

1. Body scan: Similar to the body scan meditation, this technique involves lying down and systematically scanning the body from head to toe, focusing on each part and its sensations. However, during a body scan for mindful movement, one incorporates slow, deliberate movements into the process.

2. Mindful walking: Walking can be a great form of mindful movement when done with awareness. Instead of walking mindlessly, one can focus on the sensations in the feet, legs, and body as they take each step. It is recommended to walk slowly and deliberately, taking notice of the surroundings and being present in the moment.

3. Yoga: As mentioned earlier, yoga can be an effective form of mindful movement. It combines physical postures, breathing techniques, and meditation, which can help to increase body awareness and reduce stress. There are various styles of yoga, such as Hatha, Vinyasa, and Kundalini, that one can try depending on their needs and preferences.

4. Tai Chi: This is a traditional Chinese practice that involves slow, flowing movements and deep breathing. It is often referred to as a moving meditation and can help to reduce stress, increase flexibility and balance, and improve overall well-being.

5. Qigong: Another Chinese practice, Qigong involves slow, gentle movements and breathing techniques to promote relaxation and increase body awareness. It can be done standing, sitting, or lying down, and is suitable for people of all ages and fitness levels.

6. Dance: Dancing can also be a form of mindful movement when done with awareness. Instead of following a routine, one can allow their body to move freely and expressively, focusing on the sensations and emotions that arise.

Incorporating mindful movement into one's daily routine can have numerous benefits for physical and mental health. These techniques can be done individually or combined to create a well-rounded mindful movement practice.

Incorporating mindful movement into daily life

Incorporating mindful movement into daily life is an effective way to reduce stress and improve overall well-being. Mindful movement can be practiced in a variety of ways, including yoga, tai chi, qigong, and other forms of gentle exercise. Here are some techniques for incorporating mindful movement into daily life:

1. Start with small movements: If you're new to mindful movement, start with small movements like stretching or simple yoga poses. You don't have to do an entire yoga sequence or tai chi routine to experience the benefits of mindful movement. Even a few minutes of stretching or gentle movement can help reduce stress and improve flexibility.

2. Make it a habit: To get the most benefit from mindful movement, make it a daily habit. Find a time that works for you, whether it's in the morning, during a lunch break, or in the evening. Incorporate mindful movement into your daily routine, just like brushing your teeth or taking a shower.

3. Practice mindfulness: Mindful movement is not just about the physical movements themselves, but also about being present and aware in the moment. Focus on your breath and your body as you move, and let go of distractions

and thoughts. This can help you feel more relaxed and centered.

4. Find a class or community: Practicing mindful movement with others can be a great way to stay motivated and connect with like-minded individuals. Look for a yoga or tai chi class in your community, or consider joining an online group.

5. Use technology: If you don't have access to a class or community, there are many online resources and apps that can guide you through mindful movement exercises. From YouTube videos to apps like Headspace and Calm, there are many ways to incorporate mindful movement into your daily routine.

6. Take breaks during the workday: Mindful movement can also be incorporated into your workday to help reduce stress and improve focus. Take breaks every hour or so to stretch or do some simple yoga poses. This can help you feel more refreshed and energized.

7. Embrace nature: Mindful movement can also be practiced outdoors, surrounded by nature. Take a walk in the park, practice yoga on the beach, or go for a hike in the mountains. Being in nature can help reduce stress and promote a sense of calm and well-being.

Incorporating mindful movement into daily life can help reduce stress, improve flexibility and balance, and promote overall well-being. Whether you prefer yoga, tai chi, or another form of mindful movement, finding ways to incorporate it into your daily routine can have a positive impact on your physical and mental health.

Chapter 6: Developing Mindful Awareness
The importance of mindful awareness in stress reduction

Mindful awareness, also known as mindfulness, is the practice of being present and fully engaged in the current moment. It is the ability to pay attention to your thoughts, feelings, bodily sensations, and the environment around you without judgment. Mindful awareness has been shown to be an effective tool for reducing stress and anxiety.

Stress is a natural response to challenging situations. However, chronic stress can have negative effects on our physical and mental health. Stress can lead to increased blood pressure, heart rate, and cortisol levels, which can increase the risk of heart disease, stroke, and other health problems. Chronic stress can also lead to anxiety, depression, and other mental health issues.

Mindful awareness can help reduce stress by allowing us to observe our thoughts and emotions without judgment. When we are mindful, we can recognize when we are experiencing stress and take steps to manage it. Mindful awareness can also help us develop a greater sense of self-awareness, which can lead to better decision-making and improved relationships.

Techniques for developing mindful awareness

Developing mindful awareness takes practice. Here are some techniques you can use to cultivate mindful awareness:

1. Mindful breathing: One of the most basic and effective techniques for developing mindful awareness is mindful breathing. Simply focus your attention on your breath, noticing the sensation of air moving in and out of your body. When your mind starts to wander, gently bring your attention back to your breath.

2. Body scan meditation: Body scan meditation is a technique that involves scanning your body from head to toe, noticing any sensations or discomfort. This technique can help you become more aware of your body and any physical tension you may be holding.

3. Mindful movement: Mindful movement practices such as yoga, tai chi, or qigong can help you develop mindful awareness by focusing your attention on your body and movements.

4. Mindful eating: Mindful eating involves paying attention to the taste, texture, and sensations of food as you eat it. This can help you develop a greater appreciation for food and make healthier eating choices.

5. Mindful listening: Mindful listening involves fully focusing on the person who is speaking to you, without

interrupting or thinking about your response. This can help improve communication and build stronger relationships.

Incorporating mindful awareness into daily life

Incorporating mindful awareness into your daily life can help reduce stress and improve your overall well-being. Here are some tips for incorporating mindful awareness into your daily routine:

1. Start small: Begin by practicing mindful awareness for just a few minutes each day. Over time, you can gradually increase the amount of time you spend practicing.

2. Use reminders: Use reminders throughout the day to help you remember to be mindful. This could be as simple as setting an alarm on your phone or placing a note on your desk.

3. Practice gratitude: Take a few moments each day to reflect on what you are grateful for. This can help shift your focus away from stress and towards positivity.

4. Be present: When you are engaged in a task, try to focus all of your attention on that task. Avoid multitasking, which can lead to increased stress and decreased productivity.

5. Practice self-care: Taking care of your physical and mental health is an important aspect of mindful awareness.

Make sure to get enough sleep, exercise regularly, and eat a healthy diet.

Techniques for developing mindful awareness

Mindful awareness is the ability to pay attention to the present moment in a non-judgmental and accepting way. Developing mindful awareness involves cultivating the ability to observe thoughts, feelings, and bodily sensations without becoming overwhelmed or reactive. There are many techniques that can be used to develop mindful awareness, including the following:

1. Mindful breathing: Mindful breathing is the practice of focusing on the breath as a way to develop concentration and awareness. This involves paying attention to the sensations of the breath as it moves in and out of the body. When the mind wanders, gently bring it back to the breath.

2. Body scan meditation: Body scan meditation involves paying attention to the sensations in different parts of the body. This technique can be practiced lying down or sitting up, and involves systematically scanning the body from head to toe, bringing awareness to any areas of tension or discomfort.

3. Mindful movement: Mindful movement practices, such as yoga or tai chi, can help develop mindful awareness by bringing attention to the present moment through movement. These practices involve paying attention to the

sensations in the body as it moves through different postures or movements.

4. Mindful eating: Mindful eating involves paying attention to the experience of eating, including the taste, texture, and sensations in the body. This technique can be practiced by taking time to eat slowly, savoring each bite, and paying attention to the physical sensations of hunger and fullness.

5. Mindful walking: Mindful walking involves paying attention to the sensations in the body as it moves through space. This technique can be practiced by walking slowly and deliberately, paying attention to the movement of the feet, the sensations in the legs, and the environment around you.

6. Mindful listening: Mindful listening involves paying attention to the sounds around you, without judgment or distraction. This technique can be practiced by focusing on the sounds of nature, music, or even everyday noises, such as the sound of the wind or the hum of a refrigerator.

7. Mindful observation: Mindful observation involves paying attention to the environment around you, without judgment or distraction. This technique can be practiced by observing the beauty of nature, the movement of people, or the changing colors of the sky.

By practicing these techniques regularly, individuals can develop the ability to stay present in the moment, without becoming distracted by thoughts, worries, or distractions. This can help reduce stress and increase feelings of calm and well-being.

It is important to note that developing mindful awareness is a gradual process that takes time and patience. It is also important to practice with a sense of curiosity and openness, rather than striving for perfection or trying to achieve a specific outcome. With regular practice and a willingness to learn and grow, anyone can develop mindful awareness and experience the benefits of being fully present in the moment.

The benefits of mindful awareness

The practice of developing mindful awareness has numerous benefits for individuals in all aspects of their lives. Here are some of the key benefits:

1. Stress Reduction: Mindful awareness is an effective way to reduce stress, as it allows individuals to recognize and respond to stressors in a healthy manner. Through practicing mindfulness, individuals learn to be present in the moment and observe their thoughts, feelings, and bodily sensations without judgment. This can help to reduce feelings of anxiety and stress.

2. Emotional Regulation: Mindfulness has been shown to improve emotional regulation, particularly in individuals who struggle with anxiety and depression. By becoming more aware of their emotions and the triggers that lead to them, individuals can learn to respond to their emotions in a more adaptive way.

3. Improved Cognitive Function: Mindfulness has also been shown to improve cognitive function, particularly in areas related to attention and memory. By practicing mindfulness, individuals may be able to improve their ability to focus and concentrate on tasks.

4. Better Sleep: Mindfulness has been linked to improved sleep quality, as individuals who practice

mindfulness may experience fewer racing thoughts and better relaxation before bedtime.

5. Increased Resilience: Mindfulness can also help individuals build resilience, or the ability to bounce back from difficult situations. Through practicing mindfulness, individuals may develop greater self-awareness and the ability to respond to challenging situations in a more flexible and adaptive way.

6. Improved Relationships: Mindful awareness can also improve interpersonal relationships. By becoming more aware of their own thoughts, feelings, and behaviors, individuals may be able to respond to others in a more empathic and compassionate way.

7. Increased Well-being: Finally, developing mindful awareness can lead to increased overall well-being. By practicing mindfulness, individuals may experience greater satisfaction with life and a greater sense of purpose and meaning.

In summary, the benefits of developing mindful awareness are numerous and far-reaching. By practicing mindfulness, individuals may experience reduced stress, improved emotional regulation, better cognitive function, improved sleep, increased resilience, improved relationships, and increased well-being.

Incorporating mindful awareness into daily life

Incorporating mindful awareness into daily life is an essential step towards living a more mindful and stress-free life. Mindful awareness is the ability to be fully present in the moment, without judgment or distraction. It involves being aware of your thoughts, feelings, and surroundings, and learning to respond to them in a way that is helpful and positive.

Here are some techniques for incorporating mindful awareness into your daily life:

1. Mindful Breathing: Breathing exercises are a great way to cultivate mindful awareness. Take a few minutes each day to focus on your breath, noticing the sensation of the air as it enters and leaves your body. When your mind wanders, gently bring your attention back to your breath.

2. Mindful Walking: Walking is another great way to practice mindful awareness. As you walk, pay attention to the sensation of your feet touching the ground, the movement of your body, and the sights and sounds around you. Notice any thoughts or feelings that arise, and simply observe them without judgment.

3. Mindful Eating: Eating mindfully involves paying attention to the taste, texture, and smell of your food, as well as your body's hunger and fullness signals. Slow down and

savor each bite, noticing the flavors and textures as you chew. Pay attention to how your body feels as you eat, and stop when you feel comfortably full.

4. Mindful Listening: Listening mindfully involves giving your full attention to the person speaking to you, without distractions or interruptions. Practice active listening by maintaining eye contact, nodding, and responding appropriately. Avoid the urge to interrupt or respond before the person has finished speaking.

5. Mindful Work: Practicing mindfulness at work can help reduce stress and improve productivity. Take short breaks throughout the day to focus on your breath, stretch, or take a quick walk. When you are working, focus on one task at a time, and avoid distractions such as email or social media.

6. Mindful Relaxation: Take time each day to relax and recharge. Practice relaxation techniques such as deep breathing, progressive muscle relaxation, or guided imagery. Engage in activities that bring you joy and relaxation, such as reading, listening to music, or spending time in nature.

Incorporating mindful awareness into your daily life takes practice and patience. Start small, with just a few minutes each day, and gradually build up to longer periods of mindfulness. With time and practice, you will begin to notice the benefits of living a more mindful and present life.

Chapter 7: Cultivating Compassion

The importance of compassion in stress reduction

The importance of compassion in stress reduction cannot be overstated. In today's fast-paced and often impersonal world, it is easy to become disconnected from our own needs and the needs of others. When we are stressed, it can be even more difficult to maintain a compassionate perspective. However, cultivating compassion can have a profound impact on our overall well-being and help us to better manage stress.

Compassion is the ability to understand and feel the pain of others, and to respond with kindness and support. It involves recognizing our shared humanity, acknowledging that we all suffer, and working to alleviate that suffering wherever possible. In the context of stress reduction, cultivating compassion can help us to approach difficult situations with greater ease, respond to our own stress with kindness and understanding, and build stronger relationships with those around us.

One key aspect of compassion is self-compassion. This involves treating ourselves with the same kindness and understanding that we would offer to a friend in need. When we are stressed, it can be easy to fall into a pattern of self-criticism or self-blame. However, this only exacerbates our stress and makes it more difficult to cope. By cultivating self-compassion, we can offer ourselves the support and encouragement that we need to manage stress in a healthier way.

Compassion also involves cultivating empathy and connection with others. When we feel stressed or overwhelmed, it can be easy to withdraw from social interactions and become isolated. However, research has shown that social support is a critical component of stress reduction. Cultivating compassion can help us to connect with others on a deeper level, build stronger relationships, and create a support network that can help us to manage stress more effectively.

Another important aspect of compassion is altruism. This involves extending our compassion and support to others, even when it may be difficult or inconvenient. Altruism has been shown to have numerous benefits for mental health and well-being, including reduced stress and increased feelings of happiness and fulfillment. By cultivating compassion and altruism, we can create a positive ripple effect in our communities and contribute to a more compassionate and supportive society.

Overall, the importance of compassion in stress reduction cannot be overstated. By cultivating compassion for ourselves and others, we can approach stress with greater ease and resilience, build stronger relationships, and contribute to a more compassionate and supportive world.

Techniques for developing self-compassion

Self-compassion is the act of being kind and understanding toward oneself when faced with difficult situations or when making mistakes. It involves treating oneself with the same warmth, care, and understanding as one would a good friend. Developing self-compassion can be an effective tool in managing stress, improving mental health, and increasing overall well-being. In this section, we will explore some techniques for developing self-compassion.

1. Mindful Self-Compassion Meditation

Mindful self-compassion meditation is a technique that combines mindfulness and self-compassion. It involves being mindful of one's thoughts and emotions while treating oneself with kindness and understanding. This technique can be practiced by following these steps:

- Find a quiet and comfortable place where you can sit or lie down.

- Close your eyes and take a few deep breaths to relax.

- Focus on your breath, paying attention to the sensation of air entering and leaving your body.

- As you breathe, imagine that you are sending feelings of warmth and kindness to yourself.

- When you notice negative thoughts or emotions, acknowledge them without judgment or criticism.

- Treat yourself with kindness and understanding by saying compassionate phrases such as "May I be kind to myself," "May I be patient with myself," or "May I forgive myself."

- Continue this practice for 5-10 minutes.

2. Loving-Kindness Meditation

Loving-kindness meditation is a technique that involves sending positive thoughts and feelings to oneself and others. It can be an effective way to cultivate self-compassion and compassion for others. This technique can be practiced by following these steps:

- Find a quiet and comfortable place where you can sit or lie down.

- Close your eyes and take a few deep breaths to relax.

- Imagine yourself in a peaceful and safe place, surrounded by people who love and care for you.

- Focus on your breath, paying attention to the sensation of air entering and leaving your body.

- As you breathe, repeat compassionate phrases such as "May I be happy," "May I be healthy," "May I be safe," and "May I live with ease."

- After several minutes, visualize someone you care about and repeat the same phrases for them.

- Expand this practice to include others in your life, including people you feel neutral toward and people you may have difficulty with.

3. Letter Writing

Letter writing is a technique that involves writing a compassionate letter to oneself. This technique can be an effective way to acknowledge and validate one's feelings while treating oneself with kindness and understanding. This technique can be practiced by following these steps:

- Find a quiet and comfortable place where you can write without distractions.
- Write a letter to yourself, acknowledging your struggles and challenges while expressing kindness and understanding.
- Use compassionate phrases such as "I know you are struggling, and that's okay," "I want you to know that you are not alone," and "You are doing the best you can."
- Write as if you are speaking to a good friend who is going through a difficult time.
- Read the letter to yourself several times, allowing the compassionate words to sink in.

4. Mindful Self-Compassion Breaks

Mindful self-compassion breaks are a technique that involves taking short breaks throughout the day to check in with oneself and treat oneself with kindness and understanding. This technique can be practiced by following these steps:

- Set a timer for several times throughout the day.

- When the timer goes off, take a few deep breaths to relax.

- Check in with yourself and acknowledge your thoughts and feelings without judgment or criticism.

- Treat yourself with kindness and understanding by saying compassionate phrases such as "May I be kind to myself," "May I be patient with myself,"

Techniques for developing compassion for others

Developing compassion for others is an important aspect of cultivating compassion. It helps us to recognize the suffering of others and to respond with kindness and empathy. Here are some techniques for developing compassion for others:

1. Loving-kindness meditation: Loving-kindness meditation is a technique for developing compassion and kindness towards oneself and others. It involves repeating phrases of well-wishing towards oneself and others, starting with someone you love, then someone neutral, and finally someone with whom you may have difficulties. The phrases can vary but may include statements such as "May you be happy, may you be safe, may you be healthy, may you be at peace."

2. Compassionate listening: Compassionate listening is a technique that involves being present and fully attentive to someone else's experience without judgment or interruption. It involves actively listening to what the person is saying, acknowledging their feelings, and responding with empathy and kindness.

3. Practicing empathy: Practicing empathy involves putting ourselves in someone else's shoes and trying to understand their perspective. It requires us to suspend our

own judgments and biases and to truly listen to the other person's experience.

4. Engaging in acts of kindness: Engaging in acts of kindness towards others is a way to cultivate compassion and empathy. It involves intentionally doing something kind for someone else, without expecting anything in return.

5. Volunteering: Volunteering is another way to develop compassion for others. It involves giving our time and energy to help those in need, whether it's through volunteering at a local food bank or participating in a community service project.

6. Practicing forgiveness: Forgiveness is an important aspect of compassion, as it involves letting go of resentment and anger towards others. It allows us to move past our hurt and to cultivate a sense of empathy and understanding towards the person who may have wronged us.

7. Reading and learning about others' experiences: Reading and learning about others' experiences, especially those who are different from us, can help to broaden our understanding and empathy towards others. It can help us to recognize the common humanity that we all share and to develop compassion for those who may be experiencing difficulties or challenges.

Incorporating these techniques into our daily lives can help us to develop greater compassion for others, and to respond to their suffering with kindness, empathy, and understanding. Over time, this can lead to a greater sense of connection and community, and can help to reduce feelings of isolation and loneliness.

The benefits of cultivating compassion

The practice of cultivating compassion is not just a noble pursuit, but also has numerous benefits for our mental and physical well-being. When we cultivate compassion, we develop a deeper understanding of ourselves and others, and this understanding leads to greater happiness and a sense of connectedness with the world around us. Here are some of the many benefits of cultivating compassion:

1. Improved Relationships: When we cultivate compassion, we become more empathetic and understanding towards others. This allows us to develop more meaningful and satisfying relationships with the people around us.

2. Reduced Stress: Compassion can help reduce stress by promoting positive emotions, such as love and kindness, which counteract negative emotions such as anger and fear. Compassion also helps us develop better coping mechanisms, which can help us deal with stress more effectively.

3. Increased Resilience: Compassion can help us become more resilient in the face of adversity. When we cultivate compassion, we develop a greater sense of purpose and meaning, which can help us overcome challenges and bounce back from setbacks.

4. Improved Mental Health: Cultivating compassion can have a positive impact on our mental health. Research has shown that people who practice compassion meditation have reduced symptoms of depression and anxiety, and improved overall well-being.

5. Increased Happiness: Compassion can bring us a sense of joy and happiness. When we focus on the well-being of others, we create positive feelings within ourselves, which can lead to greater happiness and contentment.

6. Improved Physical Health: Compassion can have a positive impact on our physical health as well. Studies have shown that people who practice compassion have lower blood pressure, improved immune function, and reduced risk of heart disease.

7. Increased Mindfulness: Compassion is closely linked to mindfulness, and cultivating compassion can help us become more mindful in our daily lives. When we practice compassion, we become more aware of our thoughts and emotions, and develop a greater sense of presence in the moment.

8. Increased Altruism: Compassion can inspire us to become more altruistic and to help others. When we feel compassion for someone, we are more likely to want to help

them in any way we can, whether that means donating to charity or volunteering our time.

9. Improved Self-Esteem: Compassion can also have a positive impact on our self-esteem. When we focus on the well-being of others, we develop a greater sense of purpose and meaning in our lives, which can lead to greater self-confidence and self-worth.

In summary, cultivating compassion can have a profound impact on our mental and physical well-being. By practicing compassion, we can improve our relationships, reduce stress, increase resilience, improve mental health, increase happiness, improve physical health, increase mindfulness, become more altruistic, and improve self-esteem. These benefits make cultivating compassion a worthwhile pursuit for anyone looking to improve their quality of life.

Conclusion
The benefits of MBSR for mental and emotional well-being

Introduction: In recent years, mindfulness-based stress reduction (MBSR) has gained a lot of popularity as a way to reduce stress and improve mental and emotional well-being. MBSR is an 8-week program that uses various techniques such as mindful breathing, body scan meditation, mindful movement, and developing mindful awareness and compassion to reduce stress and improve overall well-being. In this chapter, we will discuss the benefits of MBSR for mental and emotional well-being.

1. Reduces Stress and Anxiety: One of the main benefits of MBSR is that it reduces stress and anxiety levels. The various techniques used in MBSR help individuals to become more aware of their thoughts and feelings, and how they react to stressful situations. This increased awareness helps them to develop a more positive outlook on life, and to cope better with stress and anxiety.

2. Improves Emotional Regulation: MBSR also helps individuals to improve their emotional regulation. By becoming more aware of their thoughts and feelings, they can better understand and manage their emotions. This can lead to a greater sense of emotional balance and stability.

3. Enhances Cognitive Function: MBSR has also been shown to enhance cognitive function. Studies have shown that MBSR can improve attention, memory, and executive functioning, which can help individuals to better focus and perform tasks more effectively.

4. Promotes Physical Health: MBSR has also been linked to a number of physical health benefits. For example, MBSR has been shown to reduce blood pressure, lower heart rate, and improve immune function. Additionally, MBSR can help to reduce pain and improve overall physical well-being.

5. Increases Self-Awareness and Self-Compassion: Through the practice of MBSR, individuals can become more self-aware and develop a greater sense of self-compassion. By learning to be more mindful of their thoughts and feelings, individuals can develop a greater understanding of themselves and their needs. This can lead to greater self-acceptance and a more positive self-image.

Conclusion: In conclusion, MBSR is a powerful tool for reducing stress and improving mental and emotional well-being. By incorporating various mindfulness techniques into their daily lives, individuals can learn to better manage stress and anxiety, improve their emotional regulation, enhance cognitive function, promote physical health, and increase their self-awareness and self-compassion. The benefits of MBSR are numerous and can have a profound impact on individuals' overall well-being.

Encouragement to continue practicing mindfulness-based stress reduction

After learning about the various techniques and benefits of mindfulness-based stress reduction (MBSR) throughout this book, it is important to acknowledge that adopting these practices into your daily routine can be a challenge. However, the benefits of MBSR for mental and emotional well-being are numerous and well-documented, making it worthwhile to continue practicing.

One of the keys to success with MBSR is to start small and be consistent. It can be overwhelming to try to incorporate multiple mindfulness techniques all at once, so it is helpful to choose one or two techniques that resonate with you and start there. For example, you may choose to practice mindful breathing or body scan meditation for just a few minutes each day and gradually increase the time as you become more comfortable.

Another important aspect of practicing MBSR is to approach it with an open and curious mindset. This means being willing to observe your thoughts and emotions without judgment or attachment, and simply accepting whatever arises in the present moment. It is natural for your mind to wander during meditation, but the key is to gently bring your focus back to your breath or body sensations and continue with the practice.

It is also helpful to find a community or support system to aid in your practice. This can include attending a formal MBSR program or finding a local meditation group. Surrounding yourself with others who are also committed to mindfulness can provide motivation and accountability, as well as opportunities for learning and growth.

In addition to formal practice, there are many ways to incorporate mindfulness into daily life. This can include taking mindful walks, practicing mindful eating, or simply being present and fully engaged in everyday activities. The more you practice mindfulness, the more it becomes a natural part of your daily routine and a way of being in the world.

Ultimately, the benefits of MBSR extend far beyond stress reduction and can have a positive impact on all aspects of life, including relationships, work, and personal growth. By committing to a regular mindfulness practice and approaching it with openness and curiosity, you can experience the transformative power of MBSR and cultivate greater peace, joy, and well-being in your life.

Further resources for exploring MBSR and mindfulness

In this final section, we will discuss additional resources for those interested in further exploring mindfulness-based stress reduction (MBSR) and mindfulness in general. Whether you are looking to deepen your practice or learn more about the theory and science behind mindfulness, there are numerous resources available to help you on your journey.

1. Books on MBSR and Mindfulness

There are many books available on the topic of MBSR and mindfulness that can provide additional guidance and insights into the practice. Some popular books include:

- "Full Catastrophe Living" by Jon Kabat-Zinn: This book is often considered the "bible" of MBSR, written by the creator of the program himself. It offers a comprehensive guide to the practice of mindfulness and how it can be applied to various areas of life.

- "Mindfulness: A Practical Guide to Finding Peace in a Frantic World" by Mark Williams and Danny Penman: This book offers a step-by-step guide to MBSR, with practical exercises and meditations to help you develop your mindfulness practice.

- "The Power of Now" by Eckhart Tolle: While not specifically about MBSR, this book offers a powerful message about the importance of living in the present moment and letting go of negative thoughts and emotions.

2. Online Courses and Programs

For those who prefer a more structured approach to learning, there are numerous online courses and programs available that can help you deepen your understanding and practice of mindfulness. Some popular options include:

- Mindful.org: This website offers a variety of online courses and programs on mindfulness, including an eight-week MBSR course.

- Headspace: This app offers guided meditations and mindfulness exercises for beginners and more experienced practitioners alike.

- The Mindfulness-Based Stress Reduction Online Course: This online course is based on the same curriculum as the in-person MBSR program and is led by experienced teachers.

3. Mindfulness-Based Therapy

In addition to MBSR, there are several other mindfulness-based therapies that may be helpful for those struggling with anxiety, depression, or other mental health issues. These therapies are often based on the same principles as MBSR but are tailored to address specific issues or conditions. Some popular mindfulness-based therapies include:

- Mindfulness-Based Cognitive Therapy (MBCT): This therapy combines mindfulness practices with cognitive-behavioral therapy techniques to help individuals manage symptoms of depression and anxiety.

- Acceptance and Commitment Therapy (ACT): This therapy uses mindfulness practices to help individuals accept difficult thoughts and feelings and take action towards their values and goals.

- Dialectical Behavior Therapy (DBT): This therapy combines mindfulness practices with other behavioral and cognitive techniques to help individuals manage difficult emotions and improve their relationships with others.

4. Mindfulness Retreats

For those looking for a more immersive experience, mindfulness retreats can provide an opportunity to deepen your practice and connect with other like-minded individuals. These retreats can range from weekend workshops to multi-week programs and are often held in beautiful, peaceful settings. Some popular mindfulness retreats include:

- Insight Meditation Society: This center offers a variety of retreats and programs based on Buddhist teachings and mindfulness practices.

- Omega Institute: This wellness center offers a variety of retreats and workshops on mindfulness, meditation, and yoga.

- Shambhala Mountain Center: This retreat center offers a variety of programs on mindfulness, meditation, and other contemplative practices.

Conclusion

Whether you are just beginning your mindfulness journey or are looking to deepen your practice, there are numerous resources available to help you along the way. From books and online courses to mindfulness-based therapies and retreats, there is no shortage of ways to learn and grow in your practice. Remember that mindfulness is a lifelong journey, and the more you practice, the more benefits you are likely to experience. Don't be discouraged if you encounter challenges along the way, as mindfulness is not about perfection but rather about cultivating awareness and acceptance in the present moment.

One valuable resource for further exploration of mindfulness-based stress reduction (MBSR) is the Center for Mindfulness at the University of Massachusetts Medical

School, where the program was originally developed. They offer a variety of MBSR courses and retreats for individuals and healthcare professionals, as well as online resources such as guided meditations and mindfulness exercises. Additionally, there are many other organizations and individuals who offer MBSR programs and resources, including trained MBSR instructors and therapists.

Books can also be a great way to deepen your understanding and practice of mindfulness. Some recommended books on MBSR and mindfulness include "Full Catastrophe Living" by Jon Kabat-Zinn, "The Mindful Way Workbook" by John Teasdale, "Wherever You Go, There You Are" by Jon Kabat-Zinn, and "The Miracle of Mindfulness" by Thich Nhat Hanh.

Online courses and apps can also be a convenient and accessible way to continue your mindfulness journey. Popular options include the Mindfulness-Based Stress Reduction course offered by Sounds True, the Headspace app, and the Insight Timer app, which offers guided meditations from a variety of teachers.

In summary, there are many resources available to support your practice of mindfulness-based stress reduction and mindfulness in general. Remember to approach your practice with openness, curiosity, and patience, and to be kind and compassionate with yourself along the way. With consistent practice and a willingness to learn and grow, mindfulness has the potential to greatly improve your mental and emotional well-being, and enrich your life in countless ways.

THE END

Wordbook

Welcome to the glossary section of this book. Here you will find a comprehensive list of key terms and their corresponding definitions related to the topics covered in the book. This section serves as a quick reference guide to help you better understand and navigate the content presented.

1. Mindfulness: The practice of being fully present and engaged in the current moment, without judgment or distraction.

2. Stress: A physiological and psychological response to internal or external demands that exceed an individual's coping resources.

3. Meditation: A practice that involves training the mind to focus and calm the body, often through specific techniques such as breathing exercises or visualization.

4. Mind-body connection: The idea that the mind and body are interconnected and influence each other, with the health of one impacting the health of the other.

5. Yoga: A physical and spiritual practice that involves a series of postures and breath control techniques to promote physical and mental well-being.

6. Compassion: The ability to empathize with others and feel a deep concern for their well-being, often leading to actions that benefit others.

7. Self-compassion: The ability to extend compassion to oneself, treating oneself with kindness and understanding in the face of suffering or failure.

8. Awareness: The state of being conscious and mindful of one's surroundings, thoughts, and emotions.

9. Mindfulness-based stress reduction (MBSR): A structured program that uses mindfulness meditation and other techniques to help individuals manage stress and promote overall well-being.

Supplementary Materials

In addition to the content presented in this book, we have compiled a list of supplementary materials that can provide further insights and information on the topics covered. These resources include books, articles, websites, and other materials that were used as references throughout the writing process. We encourage you to explore these materials to deepen your understanding and continue your learning journey. Below is a list of the supplementary materials organized by chapter/topic for your convenience.

Introduction

- Kabat-Zinn, J. (2013). Full catastrophe living: Using the wisdom of your body and mind to face stress, pain, and illness (Revised edition). Bantam Books.

Chapter 1: Understanding Stress

- McEwen, B. S. (2017). Neurobiological and systemic effects of chronic stress. Chronic stress (Thousand Oaks, Calif.), 1, 2470547017692328.

- Sapolsky, R. M. (2004). Why zebras don't get ulcers: An updated guide to stress, stress-related diseases, and coping. Holt Paperbacks.

Chapter 2: The MBSR Program

- Kabat-Zinn, J. (2013). Full catastrophe living: Using the wisdom of your body and mind to face stress, pain, and illness (Revised edition). Bantam Books.
- Santorelli, S. (1999). Heal thy self: Lessons on mindfulness in medicine. Harmony Books.

Chapter 3: Mindful Breathing Exercises

- Kabat-Zinn, J. (2013). Full catastrophe living: Using the wisdom of your body and mind to face stress, pain, and illness (Revised edition). Bantam Books.
- Siegel, D. J. (2010). The mindful therapist: A clinician's guide to mindsight and neural integration. WW Norton & Company.

Chapter 4: Body Scan Meditation

- Kabat-Zinn, J. (2013). Full catastrophe living: Using the wisdom of your body and mind to face stress, pain, and illness (Revised edition). Bantam Books.
- Siegel, D. J. (2010). The mindful therapist: A clinician's guide to mindsight and neural integration. WW Norton & Company.

Chapter 5: Mindful Movement

- Kabat-Zinn, J. (2013). Full catastrophe living: Using the wisdom of your body and mind to face stress, pain, and illness (Revised edition). Bantam Books.

- Lynch, M. E. (2015). Mindfulness in motion: A happier, healthier life through body-centred meditation. Simon and Schuster.

Chapter 6: Developing Mindful Awareness

- Kabat-Zinn, J. (2013). Full catastrophe living: Using the wisdom of your body and mind to face stress, pain, and illness (Revised edition). Bantam Books.
- Siegel, D. J. (2010). The mindful therapist: A clinician's guide to mindsight and neural integration. WW Norton & Company.

Chapter 7: Cultivating Compassion

- Germer, C. K. (2009). The mindful path to self-compassion: Freeing yourself from destructive thoughts and emotions. Guilford Press.
- Neff, K. D. (2011). Self-compassion: Stop beating yourself up and leave insecurity behind. HarperCollins.

Conclusion

- Kabat-Zinn, J. (2013). Full catastrophe living: Using the wisdom of your body and mind to face stress, pain, and illness (Revised edition). Bantam Books.
- Siegel, D. J. (2010). The mindful therapist: A clinician's guide to mindsight and neural integration. WW Norton & Company.

www.ingramcontent.com/pod-product-compliance
Lightning Source LLC
Chambersburg PA
CBHW070435010526
44118CB00014B/2048